Y0-BQO-997

At Issue

| Banned Books

Other Books of Related Interest

At Issue

| Banned Books

Marcia Amidon Lusted, Book Editor

GREENHAVEN
PUBLISHING

Published in 2018 by Greenhaven Publishing, LLC
353 3rd Avenue, Suite 255, New York, NY 10010

Articles in Greenhaven Publishing anthologies are often edited for length to meet page
requirements. In addition, original titles of these works are changed to clearly present
the main thesis and to explicitly indicate the author's opinion. Every effort is made to
ensure that Greenhaven Publishing accurately reflects the original intent of the authors.
Every effort has been made to trace the owners of the copyrighted material.

Cover image: Lukiyanova Natalia frenta/Shutterstock.com

Library of Congress Cataloging-in-Publication Data

Names: Lusted, Marcia Amidon, editor.
Title: Banned books / edited by Marcia Amidon Lusted.
Description: New York : Greenhaven Publishing, 2018. | Series: At issue | Includes
  bibliographic references and index. | Audience: Grades 9-12.
Identifiers: LCCN | ISBN 9781534500754 (library bound) | ISBN 9781534500716
  (pbk.)
Subjects: LCSH: Censorship--Juvenile literature. | Challenged books--Juvenile
  literature. | Prohibited books--Juvenile literature. | Libraries--Censorship--Juvenile
  literature.
Classification: LCC Z657.L87 2018 | DDC 363.31--dc23

Manufactured in the United States of America

Website: http://greenhavenpublishing.com

Contents

Introduction

Book banning has a long history. For as long as books have been printed and distributed, authorities such as governments, church leaders, and family groups have attempted to suppress books that they consider as having a negative impact. Books have been banned because the ideas they contain are considered blasphemous, radical, or politically dangerous. But they have also been banned because the people or groups who object to them fear that they could create lasting harm to those who read them, especially to children.

A Long History

Book banning and censorship of the written word can be traced back to ancient civilizations such as the Greeks, Romans, and the Chinese. It was not necessarily viewed as a negative activity, since these cultures saw censorship as a legitimate way to regulate the lives of their citizens and maintain morally and politically correct behavior. At this time, governments considered it their duty to shape the moral characters of their people, and banning the written word was a part of this process.

When the printing press was invented in Europe in the fifteenth century, books were suddenly more accessible and more able to spread ideas that might not be sanctioned, especially by the Catholic Church. Printed books, for example, became a means for spreading the religious ideas of the Protestant Reformation and Martin Luther. As a result, in 1559 Pope Paul IV issued the first list of prohibited books, called the *Index Librorum Prohibitorum*, or Index of Prohibited Books. This index would be continually updated and reissued 20 more times by succeeding popes. The books in the index were prohibited because they contained heretical ideas that could be dangerous to the church. Not only were these books banned, but they were often burned, and their authors sometimes imprisoned or executed as well. The church even controlled the publication of books by universities, and no book could be printed or sold without the permission of the church. It was not until the seventeenth and eighteenth centuries, the Age of Reason in Europe, that scholars began to protest the suppression of books and ideas and the rights of free speech and free expression.

Book banning still takes place around the world, often based on the political or moral ideologies of a specific government or culture. The country of Sweden prohibits books that contain hate speech, while the United Kingdom prohibits books that contain child pornography. China's Communist government is extremely sensitive to how China's history and politics are portrayed, and may ban books that seem to criticize history or leadership or touch on sensitive political topics.

Book Banning in the United States

In the United States, book banning dates back to the passage of the Comstock Act in 1873, a federal statute passed by Congress as an "Act of the Suppression of Trade in, and Circulation of, Obscene Literature and Articles of Immoral Use." While this statute was intended to halt the mailing of materials considered to be obscene, it resulted in the banning of many books, from Chaucer's *Canterbury Tales* to Mark Twain's *Huckleberry Finn*. Even into the 1960s, books such as D. H. Lawrence's *Lady Chatterley's Lover* were still being banned under the Comstock Laws.

Today, book banning is rarely initiated by the government or religious leaders. Instead, it often comes from the public itself, such as concerned parents or organizations that are dedicated to upholding family values. Most of these campaigns take place on a state and local level, not on a wider national level, reflecting the values and concerns of particular U.S. regions and cultures. Book banning is also focused now on what is available through school and public libraries or used in classrooms, rather than focusing on limiting what the general reading public has access to. The book banning battles that now rage mostly concern which books are appropriate for children to read, based on issues such as violence, sexual content, racism, the representation of LGBTQ and mixed race characters and families, fantasy elements, and profanity. Some book banning efforts are public and receive a great deal of attention, while others are carried out quietly by teachers and librarians who remove potentially offensive books from their shelves or simply do not purchase them at all.

Currently, book banning in the United States often begins with an individual or group submitting a challenge for a particular title. A challenge is an attempt to restrict or remove materials from a library, based on the objections of that person or group, usually on moral or religious grounds. If the challenge is successful, it results in the banning, or removal, of that title. Book challenges and banning are based on the perspectives and opinions of one particular person or group, and the controversy is in the fact that banning a book removes access to it for all readers. It can also ultimately affect book publishers, booksellers, and authors, either by limiting the sale of a book or, sometimes, making it more popular as a result of notoriety.

The American Library Association (ALA), which works to uphold free access to information, created an Office of Intellectual Freedom, which receives reports from communities, the media, libraries, and schools around the country about attempts to ban books. They compile an annual list of banned and challenged books in an effort to keep the public informed about censorship that may affect them.

A Polarizing Issue

Book banning continues to be an issue that polarizes people. On one side, it can be perceived as a threat to free speech and the rights of people to access the information that they want. Banning a book can affect an entire community's ability to read a certain title. Challenging material in a textbook, which is distributed nationally, can affect the information that the entire country's children are taught. On the other side, it is seen as a means for protecting children, students, and others from content that might be considered as a threat to morals or religious beliefs or promoting negative ideas. The questions of book banning are whether it is best to suppress information that might be harmful or provocative, or if that suppression is a blow to individual rights to freedom of speech and freedom of the press. These questions are explored by the authors of the viewpoints represented in *At Issue: Banned Books*. Books, even in the age of instant information on the internet, are still very powerful means for conveying opinions, knowledge, and ideas, and so they will continue to generate controversy over whether or not they should be banned.

1

Banning and Challenging Are Two Different Things

News Staff, Business & Heritage Clarksville

Business & Heritage Clarksville is a news and business information newspaper published in Clarksville, Tennessee.

The American Library Association (ALA) maintains an Office of Intellectual Freedom, dedicated to addressing the issue of book bans and challenges. Challenging a book is the first step towards censorship and removal from libraries, but it is not the same thing as banning a book. It is also important to understand why most books are challenged, and who is doing the challenging, as well as why it has become such a controversial issue.

In celebrating the American Library Association's Banned Book Week, we at Business Clarksville took a look at why are books challenged and who the challengers are.

What is the difference between a challenge or banning?

A challenge is an attempt to remove or restrict materials, based upon the objections of a person or group. A banning is the removal of those materials. Challenges do not simply involve a person expressing a point of view; rather, they are an attempt to remove material from the curriculum or library, thereby restricting the access of others. Due to the commitment of librarians, teachers, parents, students and other concerned citizens, most challenges

"The Difference between a Ban and a Challenge Explained," by News Staff, Business & Heritage Clarksville, September 2, 2013. Reprinted by permission.

are unsuccessful and most materials are retained in the school curriculum or library collection.

Most people are well-intentioned and challenge books they see as harmful to children or which contain difficult ideas or concepts. The actions can be subtle or overt, but are still harmful. Not everyone has the same opinion, the same mindset, the same view of the world; thus in banning or challenging a book, one is depriving another of the right to read that book. We have the right as parents to our opinion and that includes an opinion about what we want our children to read. That does not supercede what other parents might want their children to read, experience and explore.

Often challenges are motivated by a desire to protect children from "inappropriate" sexual content or "offensive" language. The following were the top three reasons cited for challenging materials as reported to the Office of Intellectual Freedom:

- the material was considered to be "sexually explicit"
- the material contained "offensive language"
- the materials was "unsuited to any age group"

Although this is a commendable motivation, Free Access to Libraries for Minors, an interpretation of the Library Bill of Rights (ALA's basic policy concerning access to information) states that, "Librarians and governing bodies should maintain that parents— and only parents—have the right and the responsibility to restrict the access of their children—and only their children—to library resources." Censorship by librarians of constitutionally protected speech, whether for protection or for any other reason, violates the First Amendment.

As Supreme Court Justice William J. Brennan, Jr., in *Texas v. Johnson*, said most eloquently:

> If there is a bedrock principle underlying the First Amendment, it is that the government may not prohibit the expression of an idea simply because society finds the idea itself offensive or disagreeable.

If we are to continue to protect our First Amendment, we would do well to keep in mind these words of Noam Chomsky:

> If we don't believe in freedom of expression for people we despise, we don't believe in it at all.

Or these words of Supreme Court Justice William O. Douglas ("The One Un-American Act." Nieman Reports , vol. 7, no. 1, Jan. 1953, p. 20):

> Restriction of free thought and free speech is the most dangerous of all subversions. It is the one un-American act that could most easily defeat us.

But who are the people who challenge books?

Throughout history, more and different kinds of people and groups of all persuasions have attempted—and continue to attempt—to suppress anything that conflicts with or anyone who disagrees with their own beliefs.

In his book *Free Speech for Me—But Not for Thee: How the American Left and Right Relentlessly Censor Each Other*, Nat Hentoff writes that "the lust to suppress can come from any direction." He quotes Phil Kerby, a former editor of the Los Angeles Times, as saying, "Censorship is the strongest drive in human nature; sex is a weak second."

According to the Challenges by Initiator, Institution, Type, and Year, parents challenge materials more often than any other group.

The ALA's Office for Intellectual Freedom (OIF) receives reports from libraries, schools, and the media on attempts to ban books in communities across the country. They compile lists of challenged books in order to inform the public about censorship efforts that affect libraries and schools. The ALA condemns censorship and works to ensure free access to information. For more information on ALA's efforts to raise awareness of censorship and promote the freedom to read, please explore Banned Books Week.

2

Even Librarians Ban Books

Scott DiMarco

Scott R. DiMarco is Director of Library and Information Resources at Mansfield University of Pennsylvania. He writes about censorship and banned books, as well as library safety and security.

There are many reasons why books are challenged, and librarians are trained by the American Librarian Association in how to handle challenges in their communities. However, many people do not understand the implications of banning a book or what happens once the machinery of challenging a book is set into motion. In this case, to bring attention to Banned Books Week and the issue itself, a librarian intentionally created a book challenge situation in order to demonstrate to the community how book banning can escalate.

I n the library world, access to information is a human right, not to be tampered with or controlled in any way.

The books that line the shelves have been carefully selected by a trained librarian to offer the reader a balanced approach to all topics – that is, we try to provide all points of view, whether or not we personally agree with them.

While this may anger some people and some groups, a balance in points of view is what any good library finds essential. Occasionally, some offended person asks to have a title withdrawn from being used, which is called a "challenge"; occasionally, these challenges are successful.

Personally, I know very well what happens when a book is banned locally – because I banned one. I am a librarian and academic library director and an ardent supporter of free speech and democracy, but in 2012 I banned a book at Mansfield University of Pennsylvania.

But before I get into the story of why I banned a book, it's important to briefly touch on how often this sort of event happens – even in a land of "liberty and freedom for all."

In times of mourning or conflict – when emotions are running high and fear is pervasive – people are more amenable to having their civil liberties restricted. Look no further than the Boston Marathon bombings in 2013: in the aftermath, militarized police searched the homes of citizens without warrants, while armored vehicles roamed the streets of greater Boston.

Later, when *Rolling Stone* magazine published a photo of bomber Dzhokhar Tsarnaev on the cover, several major retail chains refused to sell the issue, claiming it to be insensitive and in poor taste. One could argue a responsible approach would have been to allow the consumer the choice of buying it or not; however, many in New England were not given this option.

These incidents present two different types of restrictions – one dealing with unlawful search and seizure, the other dealing with the role of a free press.

Nonetheless, it's a real tension in our democracy. Rights get restricted in the name of "safety" or "anti-terrorism." Whether it's magazine covers or books, year after year things get censored or banned.

For this reason, every September since 1982, libraries and similar organizations have celebrated our freedom to read with Banned Books Week, which fights for the challenged titles.

According to the American Library Association (ALA), since 1982 more than 11,300 books have been challenged for various reasons (being sexually explicit, being racially or religiously offensive, using offensive language, being unsuited for a certain age group, promoting a homosexual agenda, violence, among others). In 2014, there were 311 challenges reported to the ALA's Office of Intellectual Freedom in 2014. Many more go unreported.

Several titles are consistently challenged for any number of reasons. They range from the classics to the obscure, from required reading to graphic novels. They include Sherman Alexie's *The Absolutely True Diary of a Part–Time Indian*; Toni Morrison's *The Bluest Eye*; Justin Richardson's *And Tango Makes Three*; Dee Brown's *Bury My Heart at Wounded Knee*; Harper Lee's *To Kill a Mockingbird*; and Jack London's *The Call of the Wild*.

In 2012, some staff members and I at the Mansfield library sought to put together a week of programming during Banned Books Week to raise awareness about the many popular titles being banned at libraries around the country.

But the turnout was meager; for our panel discussion, only six people showed up.

Was the turnout low because people didn't think it was a big deal? Or were they simply not aware of how pervasive the practice was in other parts of the country? On a whim, I decided to see how locals would respond if a book was banned in their community. I wanted to bring attention to the arbitrary nature – and ease – with which this can happen.

The book we settled on was a thriller titled *One Woman's Vengeance*, written by a well-liked, local author named Dennis R Miller (who gave the social experiment his full blessing). While the book does have its fair share of sex and violence, I wanted to show that anything can be cherry-picked from a book as grounds for a challenge or ban.

I made the announcement with a simple, two-sentence memo written on official letterhead, which I posted on the library's Facebook page.

The reaction from students, faculty, alumni and the public was unexpected – and swift – in its vehemence.

Local press contacted Miller within 20 minutes of the posting; within a day, a Facebook protest page was created, an outlet for people to voice their often emotional reactions and concerns.

While the feedback was near-deafening at times, I was disappointed that on a campus of roughly 3,000 students and faculty, only eight people actually asked to meet with me to discuss the reasons I banned the book, and to ask what could be done to reverse the ban.

The overwhelming number of comments were complaints about how they felt betrayed by this action or their frustration with the administration. Some used Facebook as a forum to make rude comments from the relatively safe distance social media provides.

But efforts to get the book removed from the banned list should have been the real result. Regardless, we certainly brought the issue to the forefront of the community's collective conscience, touching a nerve many probably didn't even think they had.

While we now have several trivial and frivolous national events such a as National Coffee Day or Talk Like a Pirate Day, events that bring attention to real issues – like Banned Book Week – are too often overlooked.

Ultimately, a banned book cuts at the heart of what makes a free democracy work. As Noam Chomsky said during a 1992 BBC interview, "If we don't believe in freedom of expression for people we despise, we don't believe in it at all."

3

Do the Reasons for Banning Books Stack Up?

Jamie Leigh

Jamie Leigh is an award-winning writer based in New York City. Her published works on literature, travel, and pop culture have appeared in magazines, blogs, anthologies, and webzines in the U.S. and abroad. A lifelong book addict with the shelf to prove it, Jamie followed up a triple major in Linguistics, French, and Comparative Literature at Purdue University with an MA in Applied Linguistics at the University of London, Birkbeck College.

Is there ever a good reason to ban a book? To those who challenge books, their reasons are important, usually with an element of desiring to protect children and adult readers from moral issues or content that contains profanity, violence, or graphic sexuality. While these reasons may seem exemplary and admirable in themselves, there are often repercussions stemming from banning books whose content might be considered harmful. Banning a book based on content that might seem clearly objectionable is simply addressing a representation of an issue when perhaps the issue itself should be dealt with openly.

"10 Reasons for Banning Books, and 5 Much Better Reasons Not To," by Jamie Leigh, *Well Done Marketing*, September 18, 2014. Reprinted by permission.

B anned Books Week 2014 fast approach-eth, marching to the cadence of its creed "Thou shalt not inhibit free speech."

An annual celebration of the freedom to read, Banned Books Week was launched in 1982 to raise awareness around censorship. In its 32-year history alone, over 11,000 books have been challenged.

The vast majority of challenges to reading material, according to the American Library Association (ALA), are made by parents. Libraries, classrooms, and workplaces across the nation see attempts to ban books on a regular, if not frequent, basis; Joan Bertin, Executive Director of the National Coalition Against Censorship, encounters an attempt at book banning or censorship every week. Banned books range from contemporary bestsellers to centuries-old classics, from fictional narratives to historical non-fiction, and from children's fairy tales to adult erotica.

Fortunately, committed librarians, teachers, parents, students, and other citizens have risen to these challenges with appeals of their own, and most challenges never result in a ban. But when they do? It's usually for predictable reasons. Here are ten reasons why books are routinely banned or challenged, followed by five (much better) reasons that books of all kinds should be defended and preserved.

Off we go into the murky mindset of those who would take away our beloved stories and fictional best friends. Banned books typically include one of the following "poisonous" ingredients:

1. Racial Themes

Scores of books, from *To Kill a Mockingbird* to *The Absolutely True Diary of a Part-Time Indian*, have been banned for exploring racial themes or depicting acts of racial discrimination. The N-word is, in fact, a one-way ticket to book bonfires, even if the whole point of your book is to condemn or deconstruct racism.

Because if we all pretend a problem doesn't exist, it usually goes away on its own. Right?

2. Alternative Lifestyles

Unless a book aligns strictly with narrow conservative values, it has probably been banned somewhere, at some point—but more likely many places, many times. So-called alternative lifestyles and "deviant" behaviors that prompt libraries, schools, and businesses to ban books include drug use, fornication, and homosexuality.

Brideshead Revisited and *The Outsiders* are two such examples. And then there's *Go Ask Alice*—the most frequently banned book in high school libraries, largely due to its depiction of drug use. The challengers really missed the point on this one, though: *Go Ask Alice* unflinchingly (and, perhaps, a bit exaggeratedly) illustrates the *negative* consequences of drug use, including but not limited to homelessness, rape, prostitution, insanity, and, eventually, death.

3. Profanity

In 1977, the Ku Klux Klan—yes, *that* Ku Klux Klan—took moral issue (!) with the obscenities in *Of Mice and Men* and demanded the book be a) removed from school libraries in South Carolina, and b) burned. Other books challenged or banned for profanity include *The Great Gatsby* and *As I Lay Dying*.

This category, by the way, also covers blasphemy—because if it offends God, it also offends a lot of his admirers. *The Grapes of Wrath* stirred up trouble in North *and* South Carolina for "taking the Lord's name in vain." Now, if it were me, I would skip the trouble and paperwork of formally challenging the shameless sacrilege in this Pulitzer Prize winner, and just let God do his smiting (sorry, Steinbeck). But not all of us are rational, and not all of us have much to do on a Monday afternoon.

4. Sex

To cover all our bases, I should amend the above to include not just graphic sexual content, but also dialogue of a sexual nature, any and all references to reproductive acts, and even the barest, briefest, Disney-approved sensuality. But you get the picture.

Throughout the 1980s, *A Farewell to Arms* was banned by school officials in New York, Texas, and South Carolina—oh, and branded a "sex novel"—despite the absence of any explicit sex scenes. Apparently it doesn't bother them to share hobbies with Hitler, who also banned the book in 1933 after yet another tantrum. People weren't quite warming up to Nazi Germany yet, it seemed, so he sent his minions into libraries and bookstores across the country to seize anything that would make for good bonfire material. Coincidentally (*not*), the books deemed most incendiary were those that threatened the Nazi ideology. We can only assume all that propaganda went down easier with a little bratwurst, roasted over the dead words of Ernest Hemingway.

Sexual content was actually the top reason cited for book challenges over the last decade, probably because sex is the most dangerous, self-destructive weapon available to humanity… or something. Definitely something.

Let me leave you with this delicious morsel: In 1980, *Brave New World* was banned in classrooms by some individuals with *keen* and *discerning* foresight for "making promiscuous sex look like fun."

5. Violence

The board of education in Strongsville, Ohio, was pressured with a lawsuit in 1974 to ban *One Flew Over the Cuckoo's Nest*. The complaints of the challengers were long and varied, but mostly came down to violence: The book, in their opinion, "glorifies criminal activity, has a tendency to corrupt juveniles, and contains descriptions of bestiality, bizarre violence, and torture, dismemberment, death, and human elimination." No one apparently found the lobotomy controversial, but challengers in a Washington high school district did take issue with the book's endorsement of secular humanism.

Beloved has been banned for violence (to be fair, there's a *tiny* little bit of infanticide), and *Lord of the Flies* has seen similar treatment.

Speaking of *Lord of the Flies*…

6. Negativity

Some books are just too *sad* for us to suffer through, according to the book challengers who walk among us. Why agonize over harsh realities—or, you know, *fiction*—when we can shift our attention to raindrops on roses, and whiskers on kittens? And, of course, Prince George?

Book challengers at a North Carolina high school in 1981 were apparently willing to overlook the violence depicted in *Lord of the Flies*, but they did take issue with its negativity. They described the book as "demoralizing inasmuch as it implies that man is little more than an animal."

I try not to be the bearer of truth bombs, but *someone* needs to say it: Humans *are* animals, you North Carolinian emotional cowards, and this might not come as a surprise if your mothers hadn't pulled you out of freshman year biology because the textbook depicted skeletons *in the nude*. Also, "demoralizing"? You know what I find demoralizing? Book banning. Cheese substitutes. The Teletubbies.

And as long as we're on the subject, *The Diary of a Young Girl* by Anne Frank was banned in Alabama for being a "downer." We are talking about the true story of a teenage girl who *hid from the Nazis in an attic space in Amsterdam and wrote in her diary, "In spite of everything, I still believe that people are really good at heart."* You, Alabama, are the downer.

7. Witchcraft

OK, it's Honesty Hour. Tell the truth: After reading the first *Harry Potter*, did you or did you not pick up a pencil and try out a few spells, just to see if something would happen? Really, really hoping against hope that it would? Because, well, I did. And then, just as quickly, I got over my witchcraft "phase" and moved on with my life.

Some people think that fictional witchcraft is so harmful that any and all references to it must be eliminated—presumably by, er, witchcraft, because man, it is *everywhere*. The *Harry Potter* books, which have sold 450 million copies, are actually the most banned books in America. *The Lord of the Rings* was banned as "satanic" even though Tolkien was a devout Catholic and viewed it as a "fundamentally religious and Christian work." (It has wizards, yes, but no *gay* wizards.) Even *Sleeping Beauty* has been challenged on counts of witchcraft.

Moral of the story: Magic is *inherently evil*, even if you only use it for good. Makes sense.

8. Unpopular Religious Views

Many a book has been banned because it contained religious notions that "might not coincide with the public view." Because apparently the public view is… unanimous?

Books in this category include everything from *The Da Vinci Code*, which addresses controversial issues in Christianity, to *The Satanic Verses*, which was read as a criticism of Islam and led to assassination attempts on Salman Rushdie, his publishers, and his translators.

Religious groups, though, are notoriously hard to please. On the one hand, you have the Christians who revere *The Chronicles of Narnia* because it's a transparent, *totally* unsubtle Biblical allegory (seriously, the lion might as well have been named Jeezis). On the other hand, you have the Christians who condemn it as an attempt to "animalize" Christ. (Yes, it really has been banned for exactly that reason.) What's a magical wardrobe enthusiast to do, I ask you?

9. Unpopular Political Views

Fascism was never the cool kid in high school, and there's nary a good day to be a communist in America. Book banning based on "dangerous" political themes has been routine for a good long while.

Everything Orwellian (but mostly *1984* and *Animal Farm*) has been banned because "Orwell was a communist." (He was a democratic socialist.) Challengers in Long Island called *Slaughterhouse-Five* "anti-American, anti-Catholic, anti-Semitic, and just plain filthy." And *Of Mice and Men* drew criticism in Tennessee because Steinbeck was "very questionable as to his patriotism" and "known to have had an anti-business attitude." Sooo, case in point, amirite?

10. Unsuitability for a Particular Age Group

Some books are ultimately deemed inappropriate for their target demographic. *The Giver*, and its dark(ish) themes, is often challenged as unsuitable for children or young adults, along with *The Perks of Being a Wallflower* and *Are You There God? It's Me, Margaret*.

But withholding these books from their target audience begs the question: When *is* the best time to confront young adult issues such as puberty and bullying, if not during young adulthood?

The Catcher in the Rye has had the special privilege of being banned for almost all of the reasons listed above. Parents have objected to the book's "profanity," "lurid passages about sex," "immorality," "excessive violence," "negativity," "communist" elements (I kid you not), and depiction of alcohol abuse—criticisms guaranteed to discourage readers up to and including Rod and Todd Flanders from perusing this angsty, much-beloved classic.

And then there are the books challenged for reasons bordering on the ludicrous:

- In 1985, Shel Silverstein's *A Light in the Attic* was challenged at an elementary school in Wisconsin because it "encourages children to break dishes so they won't have to dry them."
- *The Wonderful Wizard of Oz* came under fire for depicting women in non-traditional roles, undermining the conventional view that women could not possibly serve as competent fairy tale archetypes.
- A Texas school district banned *Moby Dick* in 1996 because, bafflingly, it "conflicted with their community values."
- *My Friend Flicka*, a children's horse drama, was challenged because "a female dog was referred to as a 'bitch' in the text."
- In 2010, Merriam Webster's dictionary was banned from classrooms in southern California for defining "oral sex."

Notice that not one of the above justifications for book banning referred to "statistics," "research," or any other form of meaningful evidence that these controversial themes are harmful to us. That's because, at the end of the day, challenges to reading material come down to personal opinions. With this in mind, let's take a look at some of the reasons we *shouldn't* ban books:

1. You may not like something, but that's no reason to take it away from everyone.

The ALA's website reads like an ode, or a hymn, dedicated to free speech. Along with John Stuart Mill, Noam Chomsky, and Phil Kerby, they quote Supreme Court Justice William J. Brennan, Jr., in *Texas v. Johnson*:

> If there is a bedrock principle underlying the First Amendment, it is that the government may not prohibit the expression of an idea simply because society finds the idea itself offensive or disagreeable."

Hallelujah, Your Honor.

The crux of the matter, when it comes to censorship, is that one individual disagreement—or even widespread dispute—over an idea or form of expression does not justify its restriction. A parent may prefer to regulate their own child's reading, but that doesn't grant them the right to make decisions for *all* parents on behalf of *all* children.

With so many book challenges arising every day across the nation, it's not the children who need safeguarding; it's the books. Which brings me to reason number two.

2. "Protecting" children from the difficult realities of the world is an exercise in futility—and privilege.

If your child's first encounter with profanity is an eleventh-grade reading assignment, or if their exposure to violence is limited solely to *The Hunger Games*, I have to assume you've withdrawn from society to live in the woods at the mercy of bears. In which case, how and why are you reading this?

In a media-flooded world, where information travels exactly as fast as your Twitter feed loads, it's impossible to keep the unpleasant facts of reality at bay. And, more importantly, these naked truths *don't traumatize young people*. By cracking open a book, children are cracking open their minds. Just ask Sherman Alexie, author of *The Absolutely True Diary of a Part-Time Indian*:

> Almost every day, my mailbox is filled with handwritten letters from students—teens and pre-teens—who have read my YA book and loved it. I have yet to receive a letter from a child somehow debilitated by the domestic violence, drug abuse, racism, poverty, sexuality, and murder contained in my book.

Attempts to shield kids from life's sharper edges are an occupation of the privileged, for the privileged. Rainbow Rowell was reportedly devastated when Minnesotan school and public library officials un-invited her to speak to local students based on the profanity in her bestselling book *Eleanor & Park*. On her blog, she wrote:

> When these people call *Eleanor & Park* an obscene story, I feel like they're saying that rising above your situation isn't possible. That if you grow up in an ugly situation, your story isn't even fit for good people's ears. That ugly things cancel out everything beautiful.

The parents of children who have not experienced shattering hardships first-hand have much to be grateful for—but putting their youngsters' privilege in context, and raising their awareness of adversities faced by their peers, has immeasurable value.

3. Books are among our best teachers.

Books teach us history in context. They teach us compassion. They teach us vocabulary, and social skills, and new ways of thinking. Despite our not-so-casual saunter toward innovative, tech-based learning models, research shows that good, old-fashioned reading is still the best way to improve intelligence. Let's embrace books—not ban them—for being challenging and provocative.

You know what some of our other greatest teachers are? Teachers. So what's with the superiority complex, book banners? A group of parents in California challenged *One Flew Over the Cuckoo's Nest* back in 2000, complaining that teachers "can choose the best books, but they keep choosing this garbage over and over again." Maybe they should reexamine their logic. Teachers—a.k.a. highly trained, highly dedicated conveyor belts of knowledge—keep choosing books like *One Flew Over the Cuckoo's Nest*, and *To Kill a Mockingbird*, and *Brave New World*, over and over again, out of *all the books ever*. Is it possible that, from a professional perspective, these books are more than garbage?

I dunno. Go ask a teacher.

4. Often, the most frequently banned books are—or go on to become—celebrated classics. And that's not a coincidence.

The classics all tend to have one thing in common: They say something that humanity needs to hear, and they say it masterfully. In a multiyear exhibition, the Library of Congress named dozens of books that have shaped our heritage, from *Catch-22* to *Gone with the Wind* to *The Sound and the Fury*, each one a classic of extraordinary merit that frequently finds its way into classrooms. Classics become classics *precisely because* they confront the social, political, philosophical, and moral issues of their time, for all time, both reflecting and inspiring the most essential force of progress: critical thinking skills.

Which brings me to the last, and best, reason not to ban books:

5. Books really can change the world.

If we tried to count up all of the world's problems, we would no doubt run out of fingers. And yes, it can be tempting to drown out our neighbors' grumbles with reality TV. But if we never confront our problems, even in name, how will we overcome them? Silencing voices and stifling ideas are no means of growth, or even of shelter. In the words of the ALA, "Restriction of free thought and free speech is the most dangerous of all subversions. It is the one un-American act that could most easily defeat us."

Free expression is the weapon of enlightenment—Kafka's "axe for the frozen sea within us." Where would we be as a nation—as a planet—without the writers who dared to battle our monsters, from the mundane to the epic, with their mighty pens? *The Feminine Mystique* was the spark that ignited second-wave feminism, and *The Jungle* prompted the passage of the Pure Food and Drug Act of 1906. The foundations of evolutionary biology in Darwin's *On the Origin of Species* continue to impact scientific theory across the globe, and the Civil Rights Movement of the 1960s can find roots in *Native Son*. Never underestimate a blank piece of paper in the right hands, because words are how we live—and, for some of us, they're *why* we live.

So here's a final send-off to all the book banners who would challenge independent thought and extinguish its expression: Methinks thou doth protest too much.

4

Book Banning's Greatest Achievement Is to Reflect Our Current Culture

Clay Calvert

Clay Calvert is the Brechner Eminent Scholar in Mass Communication and Director of the Marion B. Brechner First Amendment Project at the University of Florida. He has authored or co-authored more than 130 law journal articles on topics relating to freedom of expression.

The ALA's Banned Books Week is designed to celebrate our freedom to read and the overall importance of books. But the truth is, very few books are ever truly banned in the United States, despite uproar generated by parents groups and school boards. That doesn't mean that a conscious effort should not be made to continue fighting for access to books that many believe offer some redeeming value. Beyond the emotional debates, however, looking at books that have been banned or challenged at various points in history provides us with a window to the culture of the time. Rather than providing any real resistance or danger to Americans' access to books, these objections to content teach us about the morals and standards of the time regarding sexuality, race relations, and language, among other things. Books containing descriptions of premarital sex might have been banned from libraries decades ago, but today they might only be met with protests from certain religious or family organizations. The lack of inclusion of characters of color might be a hint about race relations

"How Do Libraries Get Away with Banning Books?" by Clay Calvert, *The Conversation*, October 2, 2015. https://theconversation.com/how-do-libraries-get-away-with-banning-books-48418 Licensed under a CC BY-ND 4.0 International.

of the time. It is not only the material within the books, but the objections raised that speak volumes about our times.

Adozen years ago, in his *New York Times* review of the best-selling British novel *The Curious Incident of the Dog in the Night-Time*, Jay McInerney (of *Bright Lights, Big City* fame) called it "stark, funny and original." Told from the perspective of a 15-year-old autistic savant, the book is now a Tony Award-winning play.

But what's hot on Broadway is sometimes too hot for Florida Panhandle high schools.

This past summer, the novel was pulled from the assigned summer reading list at Lincoln High School in Tallahassee, Florida. As reported by the Tallahassee Democrat, "the move was made to accommodate offended parents," who apparently took offense to the dozens of instances of profanity in the text.

Whether it's challenging Harry Potter books for promoting Satanism and the occult or wiping *Fifty Shades of Grey* from the shelves for depicting "mommy porn," it's become all too common for books to be challenged – and sometimes banished – from local libraries and schools.

The American Library Association's annual Banned Books Week, currently in its 23rd year, officially celebrates and promotes "the freedom to read" by raising awareness of books that are most frequently challenged across the nation.

Perhaps more significantly, however, Banned Books Week also provides both a rudimentary barometer of contemporary cultural concerns – the flashpoint topics, ideas and words that push our censorial buttons – and a test of our core commitment to the First Amendment.

Beware the parental penguins

The challenged books let us take the pulse of American squeamishness and, more bluntly, intolerance. They reveal the concerns of the day that rub some people the wrong way, so much so that they take the time and effort to file complaints rather just averting their eyes or cautioning their own children.

Not surprisingly, sex and sexuality, along with religion, are hot-button topics. Number three, for instance, on OIF's list of most challenged books for 2014 is *And Tango Makes Three*. The children's book, which was inspired by actual events in New York's Central Park Zoo, tells the story of two male penguins who hatch and raise a female penguin named Tango. *Publishers Weekly* called it a "heartwarming tale."

Those challenging it, however, find it anything but heartwarming. Instead, it is "anti-family" and "promotes the homosexual agenda." Then again, at least the book was not the most challenged this past year, as it was in 2006, 2007, 2008 and 2010 (the 2014 honor goes to Sherman Alexie's *The Absolutely True Diary of a Part-Time Indian*).

Culturally, the wrath heaped upon *And Tango Makes Three* suggests that one recent Supreme Court ruling aside, we are still conflicted when it comes to same-sex marriage (apparently for both humans and penguins).

Into the courtroom

Cultural questions, of course, sometimes spill into courtrooms. While the First Amendment explicitly protects freedom of speech, it also implicitly safeguards our right to receive speech.

As Justice William O. Douglas wrote for the US Supreme Court fifty years ago in *Griswold v Connecticut*, "the right of freedom of speech and press includes not only the right to utter or to print, but the right to distribute, the right to receive, the right to read and freedom of inquiry."

Griswold's logic leads to convoluted case law surrounding public schools' ability to regulate and ban books in their libraries.

In a 1982 case called *Board of Education, Island Trees Union Free School District v Pico*, a New York school district sought to remove a number of books from library shelves, including Kurt Vonnegut's *Slaughterhouse Five*, Eldridge Cleaver's *Soul on Ice* and a Langston Hughes-edited collection called *Best Short Stories of Negro Writers.*

According to the school board, the titles removed were "anti-American, anti-Christian, anti-[Semitic], and just plain filthy."

A fractured Supreme Court wrote that "the discretion of the States and local school boards in matters of education must be exercised in a manner that comports with the transcendent imperatives of the First Amendment."

In other words, school boards have discretion to pick and choose books, but that discretion is confined by minors' rights to receive a wide swath of ideas and information, not just conformist doctrine.

US Supreme Court Justice William Brennan wrote that schools couldn't ban books 'in a narrowly partisan or political manner.' Library of Congress

The court added that "just as access to ideas makes it possible for citizens generally to exercise their rights of free speech and press in a meaningful manner, such access prepares students for active and effective participation in the pluralistic, often contentious society."

Lofty rhetoric aside, Justice William Brennan cobbled together a few rules that remain in place today: schools may not exercise their discretion "in a narrowly partisan or political manner," and they "may not remove books from school library shelves simply because they dislike the ideas contained in those books."

The court concluded there was enough evidence to suggest the school district's reasons for removal violated the principles noted above, and it denied the board's motion to have the case tossed out.

Indeed, the ALA makes it clear that despite a constant drumbeat to pull books from the shelves, "most challenges are unsuccessful and most materials are retained in the school curriculum or library collection."

Of course, a few challenges do result in bans.

Ultimately, the problem of book banning and challenging won't go away. Public libraries and schools with limited budgets must make tough calls on what to buy, remove or put behind the check-out desk. Their choices tell us much about where we stand culturally, while their willingness (for the most part) to combat challenges reflects their unwavering commitment to free expression.

5

Banned Books Week Is Propaganda

Dan Kleinman

Dan Kleinman is behind SafeLibraries, a library watchdog organization whose mission is to be a clearinghouse for information about challenging books.

The American Library Association's (ALA) Banned Books Week is meant to call attention to the issue of challenged and banned books. While it publicizes what it perceives as threats to freedom of speech and freedom of expression, its opponents often feel the annual event mocks and penalizes those who seek to challenge books for reasons that are legitimate to them. Parents, in particular, often feel ridiculed when they attempt to use the Materials Reconsideration Policies set up by the ALA to question books that are assigned to their children to read in school, even when they are complying with its process for challenging books in their communities.

The American Libraries Association [ALA] sets up parents for ridicule, then leads the charge in ridiculing them using propaganda techniques. "Banned Books Week" [BBW] is the ALA creation it uses to lead the deceptive and disgraceful effort to ridicule people. It wants people to ignore what the US Supreme Court said or even what the ALA's creator of BBW said about

"The Parent Trap: ALA Uses Banned Books Week to Ridicule Patrons Complying with ALA Materials Reconsideration Policies," *SafeLibraries*, September 29, 2010. http://safelibraries.blogspot.com/2010/09/parent-trap-ala-uses-banned-books-week.html. Licensed under CC BY 3.0 Unported.

legally keeping inappropriate material from children. The ALA cannot be trusted by local communities.

The ALA Uses BBW for Propaganda Purposes

The ALA uses BBW that it created on its own for propaganda purposes. It talks about hundreds of banned books, yet the last book banned in the USA was *Fanny Hill* in 1963, about half a century ago. For example, see "2010 Banned Books Week - Top Ten Banned and Challenged Books for 2009," by American Library Association, OIFTube, 24 September 2010.

Isn't it propaganda for the nation's self-arrogated leader in censorship to list hundreds of books "banned" in 2009 when the last book ban occurred in 1963? The goal is to convince people not to keep children from inappropriate material since that would make them "censors." What is the evidence? Read on for just the latest example.

How the ALA Sets Up Parents for Ridicule

The ALA sets up parents for ridicule. It does this by advising libraries to create, maintain, and exercise so-called "materials reconsideration policies." They should really be called "leading with the chin policies" since the ALA sets up people to get whacked merely for complying with the policy and filing a complaint as directed.

The ALA created these policies to stop the removal of books by individual librarians reacting to patron complaints by removing materials. The ALA then guides libraries on how to promote the policies to the public and the media. For example, the ALA guidance says, emphasis in original:

> What does the library do if someone complains about something in its collection? We take such concerns very seriously. First, we listen. We also have a formal review process in which we ask you to fill out a special form designed to help us understand your concerns. Anyone who makes a written complaint will receive a response in writing.

But that is patently false in spirit when viewed in context of the ALA's latest BBW propaganda. Recall the ALA propaganda I linked above:

> "In 2009, 460 books were banned or challenged in the United States," says the ALA. That may be true, but only if 460 of the 460 were challenges and not bans.
>
> "460 demands to remove books from schools, libraries and bookstores," is the next ALA statement, as shown above. Setting aside the ALA's questionable mission creep into bookstores, notice how proper filings for relief under materials reconsideration policies are characterized as "demands to remove books."

Now watch as the ALA performs the propagandistic coup of subtly claiming any and all attempts to seek compliance under the ALA material reconsideration policies are really attempts at censorship.

The ALA Ridiculing Parents

The ALA, having set up the mechanism of "materials reconsideration policies," then leads the effort in ridiculing anyone who avails themselves of the ALA-inspired policies:

> "460 persons or groups who believed that they should decide for others what they could read," says the ALA as pictured above.

So, the ALA directs libraries to utilize "Materials Reconsideration Policies," then it leads the effort to ridicule anyone who avails himself of such policies. Merely for complying with the ALA-inspired policy, you supposedly "believe you can decide for others what they could read." And all the while the ALA is in reality deciding for others what they can read, namely, anything.

The ALA goes so far as to say challenges are "a threat to freedom of speech and choice." Comply with a materials reconsideration policy the ALA recommends and you are suddenly labeled a threat to freedom of speech and choice because you supposedly believe you can decide for others what they can read. Do you understand the game the ALA is playing? Is this not propaganda?

Jamming / Ridicule = Deceptive / Disgraceful

The particular propagandistic technique being used by the ALA in this case is called "jamming" (more here: "Effect of Jamming, is achieved without reference to facts, logic or proof"). Essentially, if you ridicule everyone each time, eventually people will stop placing themselves in the position of being ridiculed.

Further, Saul Alinsky in *Rules for Radicals* said, in Rule 5, "Ridicule is man's most potent weapon. .... [Y]ou do what you can with what you have and clothe it with moral arguments." And the ALA uses ridicule for this very purpose, as a weapon to thwart efforts to legally protect children from inappropriate material. The ALA's moral argument is its BBW 2010 theme, namely, "Think for yourself and let others do the same."

See the graphic to the right for Alinsky Rule 5? See how ridicule is used to change perceptions? Is that a fair portrayal? No, it is not; rather, it is disrespectful. Similarly, is it a fair portrayal when the ALA says all "460 persons or groups ... believed that they should decide for others what they could read"? No, it is not; rather, it is disrespectful. Worse, since the ALA created the mechanism for filing complaints in the first place, its ridicule of everyone actually complying with its mechanism is particularly deceptive and disgraceful.

Does the US Supreme Court or BBW's founder have the same view as the ALA? No.

The US Supreme Court and BBW's Creator Show the ALA is Wrong

The US Supreme Court has decided some cases that imply, if not show, that book challenges can be for legitimate reasons.

US v. ALA:

> "The interest in protecting young library users from material inappropriate for minors is legitimate, and even compelling, as all Members of the Court appear to agree."

Board of Education v. Pico:

"Petitioners rightly possess significant discretion to determine the content of their school libraries. But that discretion may not be exercised in a narrowly partisan or political manner. .... Our Constitution does not permit the official suppression of ideas. .... On the other hand, respondents implicitly concede that an unconstitutional motivation would not be demonstrated if it were shown that petitioners had decided to remove the books at issue because those books were pervasively vulgar."

Even BBW's founder and former four decade de facto ALA leader Judith Krug said books may be removed from school libraries in the right circumstances:

"Marking 25 Years of Banned Books Week," by Judith Krug, Curriculum Review, 46:1, Sep. 2006:

"On rare occasion, we have situations where a piece of material is not what it appears to be on the surface and the material is totally inappropriate for a school library. In that case, yes, it is appropriate to remove materials. If it doesn't fit your material selection policy, get it out of there."

Certainly the ALA would not characterize the Justices of the US Supreme Court as censors, would it? And Judith Krug is not a threat to freedom of speech and choice because she believes she can decide for others what they can read, is she?

No. Similarly, people who file complaints in compliance with policy should not be mischaracterized by the ALA.

Conclusion

The ALA directs local libraries to create materials selection policies. It then ridicules anyone availing themselves of the policy calling them censors, threats to freedom of speech and choice, etc. It does this intentionally with the propagandistic purpose of intimidating communities into stopping or preventing in the first place efforts by community members to seek compliance with library policies, legal cases, and common sense that legally protects children from inappropriate material.

Significantly, it uses "Banned Book Week" as the focal point for aiming the ridicule at the community. The latest example of this can be seen in "2010 Banned Books Week - Top Ten Banned and Challenged Books for 2009" as discussed above.

The ALA cannot be trusted. Its propagandistic efforts are designed to fool local communities and media into leaving children exposed to inappropriate material it would be legal to prevent.

Banned Books Week is the ALA's primary vehicle for pushing this propaganda. While this may be my point of view, a simple look at the ALA policies and the latest BBW propaganda will make the point very clear. On the one hand, "We take such concerns very seriously," while on the other, the ALA obviously does not take the concerns seriously: "460 persons or groups ... believed that they should decide for others what they could read." It's the perfect "parent trap."

In the end, isn't it the ALA that's deciding what others could read? "The ... elites have convinced themselves that they are taking a stand against cultural tyranny. .... [T]he reality is that it is those who cry 'Censorship!' the loudest who are the ones trying to stifle speech and force their moral world-view on others." Please comment below.

6

Banned Books Can Be a Tool for Addressing Race

Ashley Lauren Samsa

Ashley Lauren Samsa is a freelance writer and teaches high school English in the south suburbs of Chicago.

A great deal of attention is given to banned books in terms of how their content may be morally detrimental, convey the wrong values, or be inappropriate for young readers. However, many traditionally challenged books can be used as tools for addressing issues such as racism in the classroom, under the close guidance of a teacher. Educators may present these issues in understandable, authentic language that has a greater impact on young readers than textbooks ever could. They may also be products of historic eras that students study in school, such as the Civil War or the Civil Rights Movement, and serve as valuable primary source material. Their value lies in sparking conversations about difficult topics, which is more enlightening than restricting access to them.

September 21–27, 2014, marks Banned Books Week. This year, I've decided to take a different approach to talking about banned books with my students than I usually do. Because of the unrest in Ferguson, Missouri, at the start of the school year, my students have been incredibly eager to talk about race in the United

"Using Banned Books to Address Race in Class," by Ashley Lauren Samsa, Southern Poverty Law Center, September 22, 2014. Reprinted by permission.

States. They not only want to know how our nation is handling race issues like the clash between the mostly white police force and predominantly black citizens in Ferguson, but they also want to know how our country got to where we are today.

Their desire led me to discuss in class three challenged or banned books that explicitly address racial themes and provide insight into the racial tensions of their depicted time periods; in some cases, the banning of the book was related to its historically accurate depictions of race and racism.

To Kill a Mockingbird by Harper Lee

I assign Harper Lee's classic *To Kill a Mockingbird* every chance I get. The story features Scout Finch, a young girl growing up in a small Alabama town during the Great Depression. The majority of the story centers around the court case her father, Atticus, is involved in. A lawyer, Atticus is called upon to defend Tom Robinson, a black man accused of raping and beating a poor white woman. While there is not a shred of evidence that Robinson committed the crime (and plenty that points to who did), the town generally accepts that Robinson committed the crime simply because he is black and the victim is white. As the case unfolds, readers see—through young Scout's eyes—an accurate picture of race-based injustice in the South in the 1930s.

Even though the depictions of racism are historically accurate, the book has been banned and challenged over and over because of them. In the 1980s and again from 2003 to 2009 the book was challenged repeatedly for its use of the n-word and its descriptions of institutionalized racism.*

The Adventures of Huckleberry Finn by Mark Twain

In *The Adventures of Huckleberry Finn* Twain explores contemporary (1884) moral and social justice issues through the boyhood escapades of Huck Finn and his friend, Tom Sawyer. When Huck's wayward father comes demanding money he and Tom stole, Huck ends up escaping to Jackson's Island in the middle of the Mississippi

River where he meets Jim, a runaway slave. Despite questioning the morality of helping a runaway, Huck eventually decides to help Jim. What follows is both a hair-raising adventure and a commentary on the realities of slavery.

Considering the book was first published in 1884, not long after the Civil War, it was deemed ahead of its time in its open criticism of slavery in the United States. However, the book continues to be banned in schools and libraries across the country specifically because of its use of the n-word.

Invisible Man by Ralph Ellison

Upon its publication in 1952, *Invisible Man* became an instant classic. The book follows an unnamed narrator through his childhood and college years as a black person in the South and on to Harlem, which is strikingly less racially tolerant than we might expect from the lessons in our history books. The novel was instantly praised for its accurate portrayal of racial injustice in the 1950s. The narrator is purposely unnamed to draw attention to his invisibility—an invisibility forced upon him simply because he is a black man that white people refuse to truly see. Ellison's novel has been critically admired for decades, in part for its graphic depictions of what it meant to be black during a time of great civil unrest in this country.

Unfortunately, the book has also been banned and challenged for decades. Most recently, in 2013, the book was banned in Randolph County, North Carolina, because, as the school board said, it had no "literary value." This is a ridiculous claim to make about a novel that is considered one of the best of all time and that expertly addresses complex questions of identity, diversity, justice and action against injustice.

Each of these books addresses complex race-related questions—questions our students still grapple with in today's increasingly diverse world—and the classroom is the perfect place to start talking about them.** *Invisible Man* provides many opportunities to explore issues of identity. For instance, "What does it feel like when society denies who we are?" *To Kill A Mockingbird* is ripe for justice-based questions like "How do bias and prejudice undermine equal rights?" And *Huckleberry Finn* is an ideal text for discussing the need for action in the face of injustice: "Do we have the same responsibility to act on behalf of those outside of our identity group as we do for members of our own identity groups?"

These books are only three of the great classics that show historically accurate portrayals of racism in this country. If you're looking for a way to discuss racism with your students, consider adding one of these books to your curriculum—and be sure to discuss why it is has been historically challenged so frequently. You are guaranteed to have a great discussion with your students if you do.

*While Teaching Tolerance does not support banning books or teaching editions that remove controversial content altogether, we do support teachers making informed decisions about how and when to teach difficult or potentially upsetting content. See our piece "Straight Talk About the N-Word" for more on how to facilitate conversations when teaching books like *To Kill a Mockingbird* or *Huckleberry Finn*.

**The essential questions in this blog were adapted from Teaching Tolerance's anti-bias curriculum, Perspectives for a Diverse America. You can find dozens of texts on the topic of race and ethnicity in Perspectives' Central Text Anthology.

7

Look to the First Amendment

National Coalition Against Censorship

The National Coalition Against Censorship (NCAC) is an alliance of more than 50 national non-profits, including literary, artistic, religious, educational, professional, labor and civil liberties groups. They work with community members to resolve censorship controversies without the need for litigation.

First Amendment rights and the process of book banning can be very confusing for schools and libraries. It is important to understand both the language of the First Amendment, as well as its role in public school education, when exploring the distinctions of the book challenging and banning processes. The First Amendment protects freedom of speech, but using it in an argument about censorship or challenged books can be tricky. Several court cases serve as precedents and generally lean toward the side of protecting the right to keep books in circulation.

Introduction: Free Speech, Public Education, and Democracy

The First Amendment safeguards the right of every American to speak and think freely. Its promise of freedom of expression and inquiry is important to educators and students. The First Amendment protects educators' ability to exercise their judgment in accordance with professional standards, and provides the latitude

"Censorship and the First Amendment in Schools: A Resource Guide," Online Computer Library Center, Inc., May 9, 2016. https://www.webjunction.org/documents/webjunction/ Censorship_in_Schools_Learning_Speaking_and_Thinking_Freely_The_First_ Amendment_in_Schools.html. Licensed Under CC BY 3.0 US.

to create learning environments that effectively help young people acquire the knowledge and skills needed to become productive, self-sufficient, and contributing members of society…

…Our founders recognized that public schools are a vital institution of American democracy. But education, they also knew, involved more than reading, writing, and arithmetic. Education in a democratic society requires developing citizens who can adapt to changing times, make decisions about social issues, and effectively judge the performance of public officials. In fulfilling their responsibilities, public schools must not only provide knowledge of many subject areas and essential skills, but must also educate students on core American values such as fairness, equality, justice, respect for others, and the right to dissent.

Rapid social, political, and technological changes have escalated controversy over what and how schools should teach. Issues like sexuality and profanity have raised questions for generations, but they are even more complicated now, when most school communities bring together different cultural traditions, religions, and languages. Thus, educators frequently face a daunting task in balancing the educational needs of a diverse entire student body while maintaining respect for individual rights.

The First Amendment establishes the framework for resolving some of these dilemmas by defining certain critical rights and responsibilities. It protects the freedom of speech, thought, and inquiry, and requires respect for the right of others to do the same. It requires us to adhere to Supreme Court Justice Louis Brandeis' wise counsel to resort to "more speech not enforced silence" in seeking to resolve our differences…

The Public Schools

…Public schools embody a key goal of the First Amendment: to create an informed citizenry capable of self-governance. As many commentators have observed, a democracy relies on an informed and critical electorate to prosper. On the eve of the Constitutional Convention in 1787, Benjamin Rush stated that "to conform the principles, morals, and manners of our citizens to our republican form of government, it is absolutely necessary that knowledge of every kind should be disseminated through every part of the Unites States." Not surprisingly, universal access to free public education has long been viewed as an essential to realize our democratic ideals. According to the Supreme Court in *Keyishian v. Board of Education*, 1967:

> The classroom is peculiarly the "marketplace of ideas." The Nation's future depends upon leaders trained through wide exposure to that robust exchange of ideas which discovers "truth out of a multitude of tongues, [rather] than through any kind of authoritative selection."

Schools must, of course, convey skills and information across a range of subject areas for students of different backgrounds and abilities. They must also help students learn to work independently and in groups, and accomplish all of this in a safe environment that promotes learning. Given the complexity of these responsibilities, school officials are generally accorded considerable deference in deciding how best to accomplish them.

Recent Supreme Court decisions have made it clear that the right to free speech and expression can sometimes be subordinated to achieve legitimate educational goals. (See discussions of *Hazelwood School District v. Kuhlmeier* and *Bethel School District v. Fraser*.) A school is not comparable to a public park where anyone can stand on a soapbox, or a bulletin board on which anyone can post a notice. While students and teachers do not "shed their constitutional rights to freedom of speech or expression at the schoolhouse gate" (*Tinker v. Des Moines*), speech is not quite as free inside educational institutions as outside.

This does not mean that students and teachers have no First Amendment rights at school. Quite the contrary. But within the educational setting, the right to free speech is implemented in ways that do not interfere with schools' educational mission. Students cannot claim, for instance, that they have the right to have incorrect answers to an algebra quiz accepted as correct, nor can teachers claim a right to teach anything they choose…

Distinguishing Censorship from Selection

Teachers, principals, and school administrators make decisions all the time about which books and materials to retain, add or exclude from the curriculum. They are not committing an act of censorship every time they cross a book off of a reading list, but if they decide to remove a book because of hostility to the ideas it contains, they could be. As the National Council of Teachers of English (NCTE) and International Reading Association (IRA) note, there is an important distinction between selection based on professional guidelines and censorship: "Whereas the goal of censorship is to remove, eliminate or bar particular materials and methods, the goal of professional guidelines is to provide criteria for selection of materials and methods."

For example, administrators and faculty might agree to take a discussion of evolution out of the second grade curriculum because the students lack sufficient background to understand it, and decide to introduce it in fourth grade instead. As long as they were not motivated by hostility to the idea of teaching about evolution, this would not ordinarily be deemed censorship; the choice to include the material in the fourth grade curriculum demonstrates this was a pedagogical judgment, not an act of censorship.

Not every situation is that simple. For example, objections to material dealing with sexuality or sexual orientation commonly surface in elementary and middle schools when individuals demand the material's removal with the claim that it is not "age appropriate." On closer examination, it is clear that their concern is not that students will not understand the material; rather, the objecting adults do not want the students to have access to this type of information at this age. If professional educators can articulate a legitimate pedagogical rationale to maintain such material, it is unlikely that an effort to remove it would be successful.

Of course, hardly anyone admits to "censoring" something. Most people do not consider it censorship when they attempt to rid the school of material they consider profane or immoral, or when they insist that the materials selected show respect for religion, morality, or parental authority. While parents have considerable rights to direct their own child's education, they have no right to impose their judgments or preferences on other students and their families. School officials who accede to such demands may be engaging in censorship. Even books or materials that many find "objectionable" may have educational value, and the decision about what to use in the classroom should be based on professional judgments and standards, not individual preferences. Efforts to suppress controversial views or ideas are educationally and constitutionally suspect....

...Once a school district accedes to a demand to censor, it can become increasingly difficult to resist such pressures. Once one perspective is accommodated, those with a different view come to expect similar treatment. Listening to community concerns and taking them into account in structuring the educational environment is not the same as removing material because someone does not agree with its contents. School officials always have the legal authority to refuse to censor something. They may need to do more to help members of their community understand why it is the right choice for children's education.

8

Parental Involvement Is Critical in Reading Selections

Rebecca Hagelin

Rebecca Hagelin is a columnist for The Washington Times *and the author of the book* 30 Ways in 30 Days to Strengthen Your Family.

Many people who challenge books do so out of concern for children, and feel that it is up to parents to ensure that the books their child reads are age-appropriate and do not contain topics that are potentially threatening to morality or decency. They seek to shield children from content that they are not developmentally ready for, and also to uphold the values that they and their families believe in.

While we as a society have been taught to believe that any reading is good for adolescents, it is important to consider the kinds of books that children are reading. The American Library Association (ALA), for instance, recommends books for young readers, but these recommendations reflect the organization's liberal values. Books recommended by the ALA contain curse words and graphic sexual information. In order to guarantee that a child is reading quality books—books that a parent approves of—a parent should review a child's reading material beforehand. It is a parent's responsibility—not the ALA's and not an educational institution's—to decide what a child should read.

Reading isn't always good for our kids.

How's that for an opening sentence to stir a little controversy among the educational elites?

We've been bombarded by so many messages about how reading expands the mind, excites the imagination and enhances the vocabulary (all of which are true) that many parents have forgotten that the benefit of reading for our children very much depends on what they're reading. And, I'm afraid that many children spend hours reading what often turns out to be pure rot.

With school starting all over the country between last week and just after Labor Day, it's time for a reading warning: Parents, beware.

In many cases the very liberal American Library Association exerts great influence over what reading materials teachers assign their students. But that material may be highly inappropriate for your child. Don't let the following scenario unfold in your home:

Mrs. Jones hands out a book report assignment that includes several books for her class to choose from. Mom dutifully drives Suzi to the local library and browses while Suzi selects her book. Within half an hour, book in hand, everyone is feeling rather satisfied that they have been so responsible in starting on the project early. Mom and Suzi arrive home, and while mom begins making dinner, the conscientious and responsible Suzi heads to her room and begins to consume what turns out to be highly sexualized, vulgar garbage, filled with four-letter words and enough verbal porn to embarrass even an ol' salt.

Mom doesn't have a clue that her daughter's innocence has just been molested in the privacy of her own bedroom. She won't ever know because Suzi, a bit stymied by the fact that Mom took her to get a book that her teacher assigned, will be too embarrassed and confused to ever tell. Yet, she's just had sexuality, relationships and acceptable behavior defined for her by some perverted author most folks have never heard of. And the kid was simply trying to get her homework done.

Inappropriate Books for Young Readers

While researching my book, *Home Invasion: Protecting Your Family in a Culture That's Gone Stark Raving Mad*, I took an ALA-recommended reading list for 13- and 14-year-olds to my local library and headed to the "Young Adult" section (code for "pre-teen" and "teen"). I found some books from the list; others were already checked out. One book, the librarian told me, had just been returned, but hadn't been re-shelved, so I patiently waited while she went into the back room to retrieve it.

With several items in hand, I headed back to the Young Adult section, where I couldn't help but notice pre-teen and teen girls and guys in various stages of development and maturity, dutifully searching the shelves for assigned books. I sat down on a reading bench and began flipping through the pages of the book that had just been returned.

There's something very moving about holding a book in your hand that a child has just finished reading. But the warmth in my heart soon turned into a sickening feeling in my gut when I began to read passages so cheap and trashy that I could scarcely believe my eyes. I only had to get to page four before the first of many uses of the term "motherf—" showed up. Several scenes described, in graphic detail, sexual acts between teenagers.

In the interest of decency, there's no way I can give you word-for-word examples. And I refuse to give the trashy book and its loser author free publicity in a column that often gets forwarded around the World Wide Web. I'd rather parents and other adults who care about our children and their education—and whether ... educational elites indoctrinate them in immorality—actually go to their local library and research the reading lists themselves.

Lest you think the first book was put on the list in error, the next recommended teen item I thumbed through was equally as nauseating. A sexual act between fourth-graders was a "highlight," as well as graphic details of sex between teens, including a homosexual encounter. And this is the garbage that today's educators pass off as great literature for our children? The great classics, meanwhile, are all but missing. One list I reviewed for eight-graders contained about 20 authors—none recognizable save the lone great Mark Twain. And they call this education?

The lesson here is simple. Moms and dads: Don't just naively drive your kids to the library—you must be careful to help them choose books that reflect your values. Even if your kids are in private school, you're hardly safe—many of the best schools blindly use ALA lists. Of course, if you home school your kids, you're probably already aware of the moral problems of many ALA decisions, but even if you're using a good curriculum guide, it's always best to preview the books first.

The ALA is quick to call anyone who questions its decisions a "censor." But remember, part of our responsibility and privilege as parents is to be the ones who determine what is and is not appropriate for our own children.

9

Filtering in Public Libraries Has Gone Too Far

David McMenemy

David McMenemy is a lecturer and course director for the Information and Library Studies program at the University of Strathclyde in Glasgow, Scotland. He was Editor of Library Review between 2006–2011 and is the author of The Public Library and Information Ethics: Reflection and Practice.

Censorship and banning is no longer limited to the printed word. In this age of the internet and the vast amounts of information available there, this censorship in places like libraries has expanded to include the filtering and blocking of certain websites or types of content. This prevents patrons from accessing those places on the internet. While this type of filtering was originally instituted to prevent access to explicit content, some libraries have expanded it to include content they consider to be "tasteless and offensive." Internet filtering has become the latest avenue for censorship in public and school libraries.

Τhere is nothing either good or bad, but thinking makes it so," says Hamlet upon welcoming Rosencrantz and Guildenstern to the "prison" that is Denmark. But if you're reading this from the British Library, you might have to just take my word for it.

In a classic case of internet filtering in all its glory, a wifi user at the library attempted to check a quote from Hamlet this week, only to find that access to the play had been blocked, apparently

"Hamlet Is But the Latest to Fall Victim to Library Censorship," David McMenemy, The Conversation, August 14, 2013. https://theconversation.com/hamlet-is-but-the-latest-to-fall-victim-to-library-censorship-17074. Licensed under a CC BY ND 4.0 International.

because of its violent content. There can be no clearer example of the ineptness of filtering than the words of the Bard being censored in his homeland's national library.

The library has since reinstated the Dane as an acceptable subject of inquiry but the incident speaks to concerns that have been bubbling over the past few weeks about David Cameron's plans to require UK internet users to opt in to receive pornography on their computers.

The stark reality is that internet filtering has been with us since the late 1990s in public libraries, schools, colleges and universities across the UK. It is a form of censorship we do not talk about, but let us not mince words – it is censorship. The professional body for librarians in the UK is very clear that no item should be prohibited from a library's collection except on the grounds that it is illegal within the jurisdiction to which the library is providing its service. Yet for more than a decade, libraries and other institutions have been blocking access to sites via clumsy software-driven methods that challenge the very mission they have been charged with as institutions.

Recent research conducted in our department examined the extent of filtering in Scottish public libraries. The study revealed that of the 32 public library services in Scotland, 31 filtered access to the internet on their library computers, all citing the need to block access to sexually explicit material, including images of child abuse. When queried further as to why filtering was installed, 24 of the 31 also stated that it was "to prevent access to illegal and/or inappropriate content".

Drilling down into the data to provide an understanding of exactly what this meant in reality, 18 of the library services revealed that they blocked sites classified as containing intolerance, racism, or hate, 15 barred access to sites containing violence and extremism, and 11 included sites deemed "tasteless and offensive". What begins as an arguably rational desire to protect children from harm actually grows arms and legs and reaches into areas of thought and free expression.

We should be under no illusions about Cameron's plan. If successful, it is easily tweaked at a later date to block access to other sites that are deemed inappropriate.

In the case of the British Library, the Hamlet incident highlights another issue that has become the norm in libraries across the country - the provision of services such as wifi by third-parties. As external providers normally use their own networks rather than the library networks to provide such services, they often use a different filtering system entirely from the library itself.

In some cases this means the library is not setting the filtering requirements as they would on their own network. In one local case in Scotland, access to the public library's own Twitter account was blocked within the library itself because the wifi provider automatically barred access to social networking sites.

If filtering is to become an acceptable solution to managing internet access, then we need to start a national debate on exactly what "appropriate" and "offensive" mean in the context of free expression. That filtering has been happening under the noses of the vast majority of the population, and without their input, is an unacceptable situation in a modern democracy.

Filtering may well provide an easy solution to managers and politicians who are struggling to get to grips with the technological changes that are challenging traditional notions of stewardship, information access and control, but we need much more debate and input from all citizens on what is a clumsy, inefficient, automated censorship tool and ultimately an affront to human rights.

10

Bans Distract from the Real Value of Books

Beth Younger

Beth Younger is Associate Professor of English and Women's and Gender Studies at Drake University. Her research focuses on young adult literature and feminist theory.

While many parents and educators who seek to challenge books and limit the access of students to their content do so out of concern for children, those opposed to censorship feel that limiting exposure to books that contain potentially offensive materials may actually be doing children a disservice. Censorship can create gaps in children's education, gaps that might even be harmful in themselves because it limits the information that children have to deal with those same types of difficult situations in their lives. And on a subtler note, as this viewpoint argues, restricting access to a book simply because it includes profanity or sexual situations—which young adults are exposed to from television viewing or on social media—causes them to entirely miss valuable lessons on love and acceptance, among other things.

Banned Books Week, held this year from Sept. 25 to Oct. 1, is an annual event designed to draw national attention to the harms of censorship. Created in 1982 by the American Library Association in response to a growing number of "challenged" books

"If You Want to Publish a Truly Subversive Novel, Have a Main Character Who's Fat," by Beth Younger, *The Conversation*, September 26, 2016. https://theconversation.com/if-you-want-to-publish-a-truly-subversive-novel-have-a-main-character-whos-fat-65770. Licensed under a CC BY-ND 4.0 International.

in schools and libraries, the week is really about celebrating the freedom to read.

Much of the practice of book banning takes the form of challenging a book deemed subversive and objectionable, with profanity or sexual content often the book challengers' source of ire.

These days, such campaigns can elicit an eye roll: everyone knows that teens are regularly exposed to profanity and sex online and on TV. (Rather than try to ban books, a better approach is to instead teach media literacy so young people are better able to contextualize what they're exposed to.)

The problem is that when you go after books for swears or sex, you might also be threatening books that are truly subversive: the ones that confront our unconscious biases, whether it's weight or race, and question the way we tend to think about ourselves and others. One frequently challenged book – Rainbow Rowell's 2013 young adult novel "Eleanor & Park" – does just that.

Challenged in Minnesota

"Eleanor & Park" is a romance novel about two misfits who become friends, fall in love and endure the cruelties of the world: abusive parents, poverty and bullying.

The same year it was published, a parent group in the Anoka-Hennipin school district in Minnesota tried (and failed) to get the book removed from the curriculum and school libraries. But they did manage to get the author's visit to Anoka High School canceled.

Citing 227 instances of profanity, the parents alleged that "Eleanor & Park" was "littered with extreme profanity and age inappropriate subject matter that should never be put into the hands and minds of minor children, much less promoted by the educational institutions and staff we entrust to teach and protect our children."

What are we afraid of?

Banning books in the United States is nothing new, and there's a long history of trying to prevent people (mostly kids and teens) from reading things some think they shouldn't read.

It seems that the only thing worse than sex or the "f word" in young adult literature is being a lesbian. Depicting a gay couple got copies of Nancy Garden's 1982 lesbian romance novel "Annie on My Mind" burned on the steps of the Kansas City School District headquarters in 1993.

Judy Blume's books are famous for pushing the "decency" envelope. Her 1972 novel "Forever…" is also frequently banned for sexual content and for profanity. (Pretty much yearly since its publication, "Forever…" has been challenged by Focus on the Family or The Christian Coalition.)

But there's another aspect to "Forever…" that's rarely discussed: It has a fat character who has lots of sex. Sybil is often seen as a foil to the main character Katherine, a rail-thin control freak who loses her virginity deliberately and with purpose.

Sybil is the other side of the body image spectrum: She's fat and "has been laid" by six guys. At least she gets to have sex, which is pretty uncommon for a fat girl in 1972 young adult fiction. (And there's a penis named Ralph in the book, yet another reason to read this classic.)

But "Forever…" is an extreme outlier. The way the media depicts fat characters – and fat people – has been a problem for generations. In 2011 NPR aired a piece on fat stereotypes in pop culture. The report dissected the typical fat character in TV shows and films: someone "self-loathing" and "desperate to be loved."

Of course, the lives of fat people aren't much different from those of thin people. But you wouldn't know that from the way fat bodies are portrayed on TV and in film. Research on "weight bias in the media" suggests that most representations of fat people in media are stigmatizing. More research suggests that shows like "The Biggest Loser" and "More to Love" reinforce anti-fat bias rather than fat acceptance.

We were all teenagers once

This is why "Eleanor & Park" is so refreshingly different.

Like many protagonists in young adult novels, Eleanor is a teenager who's desperate to be an adult so she can escape her awful circumstances. But while the parents trying to ban the book pounced on the profanity, they ignored one of the novel's biggest triumphs: Eleanor is fat. Yes, Eleanor is a fat female protagonist in a young adult romance novel and she's in love – she even has a cute boyfriend named Park.

As author John Green wrote in a review of the novel, "…the obstacle in 'Eleanor & Park' is simply the world. The world cannot stomach a relationship between a good-looking Korean kid and Big Red." (Big Red is Eleanor's nickname.)

Last year, Buzzfeed writer Kaye Toal penned a beautiful personal essay about discovering Eleanor in an airport bookstore. Part of what struck Toal as significant about Eleanor is that she is fat yet is not required to become thin or change in order to be loved. Despite the recent increase in fat characters appearing on television and in movies, many of them are required to change in order to be accepted. Not surprisingly, another study published in 2013 connects the prevalence of the "thin ideal" in popular literature to low self-esteem in female readers.

Letting Eleanor be fat and be loved is much needed in today's climate of "the obesity epidemic" and misplaced concerns with fatness. Park loves Eleanor; she loves him back. A simple story, but with a difference. Eleanor's fat is not really a crucial aspect of her being. She doesn't need to be fixed.

That's what makes this lovely and painful novel subversive – and what makes efforts to ban it all the more misguided.

11

Censorship Is a Loss to Culture

Afsaneh Rigot

Asfaneh Rigot works with Article 19, a London-based human rights organization founded in 1987 with a specific mandate and focus on the defense and promotion of freedom of expression and freedom of information worldwide.

Book banning and censorship in the United States is largely limited to the removal of access to materials in certain locations, such as schools and libraries. However, in other parts of the world, censorship not only controls the voices of writers. In some places, writers who address topics that might be deemed as politically or spiritually dangerous may be imprisoned or even executed. Censorship also drains a country of its culture and its literary voices.

"Censorship is the mother of metaphor" - Jorge Luis Borges.

When the Argentine writer penned this romantic interpretation of the literary strategies many resort to when faced with the prospect of totalitarian suppression, he failed to address the after-effects.

In Azad Tribune's last article, these stealthy strategies were discussed at length. Iranian artists were rightly celebrated for their ingenious methods of circumventing censorship. But what happens

"Broken Pens and Missing Pieces – the Effects of Censorship," by Afsaneh Rigot, Article19, February 27, 2015. Published with permission from ARTICLE 19

to those that suffer under the guillotine of censorship, where paths of speech and expression are blocked by unseen hands intent on muzzling free thought?

Censored art is like a puzzle with pieces missing: incomplete.

Nadine Gordimer, writer and political activist, wrote from her own personal experience that "censorship is never over for those who have experienced it. It is a brand on the imagination that affects the individual who has suffered it, forever." Through my discussions with various Iranian artists, writers and journalists over the past few months, the truth of this statement has become starkly evident.

In a report conducted by ARTICLE 19 in late 2006, the same observation was made: "The majority of the interviews – from artists in exile – provide an in-depth, textured account of the lasting effect of censorship on artistic expression and the limits that these individuals are driven to, causing them to abandon their lives in Iran." Nearly a decade later, though parliaments, presidents and policies have come and gone, this statement remains irrefutably true.

Broken Pens

"Pens which do not write for Islamic values," proclaimed Ayatollah Khomeini, "must be broken". Evidence of the Ayatollah's sincerity has been all too apparent. Disarmed of their pens, writers have been imprisoned, tortured and even executed.

Historically, writers and their pens have been in a constant state of resistance with the Iranian state. Writer and literary critique Faraj Sarkouhi, who has been involved with the press since the 1960s, has witnessed the transformation of censorship through the decades first-hand. Sarkouhi notes how censorship became more systematic in the 60s under the Shah's regime, where the Minister of Culture enforced the 'official censorship' of books, movies, music, theatre, and visual arts. This approach continued under the Islamic Republic's Minister of Culture.

However, there is a noteworthy difference in their approaches, according to Sarkouhi: "During the Shah's era, the government denied the existence of any censorship and pretended to champion the elevation and expansion of culture." By contrast, the Islamic Republic views censorship as the "religious duty of nahy az monker (preventing others from doing bad) and amre be maroof (ordering others to do good)." This stance is as open and unapologetic as it is crippling.

The lethal force of state censorship was seen most dramatically in 1981. ARTICLE 19's 2006 report outlines the crusade launched against writers and books which commenced with assaults on institutions defending freedom of expression, such as Kanoon, the Association of Writers. This campaign led to the confiscation of books; mass bonfires of literature; closure of bookshops and banning of independent publishers. Iranian culture was going up in flames.

The 90s saw a string of murders of prominent writers, murder being the most effective form of censorship. The Regime's hit list of writers consisted of 184 of the most prominent writers and intellectuals of the country.

Shedding Old Skin

Under Rouhani's administration many felt the winds of change were blowing. Many positive moves legitimised this belief, such as the relicensing of Cheshmeh, a major publishing house. Other promising statements were made in support of loosening procedures of pre-publication licensing of books and movies. This month, in Iran's 32nd ceremony of the Book of the Year Awards, Rouhani also reiterated the need to limit censorship for the good of the Islamic Republic.

Yet the Iranian Association of Writers still does not have permission to organise gatherings or officially work. In a recent interview, the cultural deputy of the Ministry of Cultural and Islamic Guidance declared that the association should "shed [its] skin" – i.e. get rid – of those dissenters against suppression and censorship, in order to get approval for this. The Association's response was simple: "If shedding [our] skin means don't say and don't write, it is never possible."

Bashing writers seems to be entrenched in the Iranian system. Two weeks ago, the poet Sepideh Jodeyri was targeted for translating French graphic novel Blue Is the Warmest Colour into Persian. This translation was seen as a promotion of homosexuality, punishable by 100 lashes or even death. She told the Guardian, "An event organised [in Tehran] for my recent poetry collection And Etc was cancelled, the organiser was sacked from his job, my publisher was threatened with having his licence suspended and interviews were withdrawn." She is now persona non grata in Iran.

Due to the internal wars of the Islamic republic, it's not uncommon for right-wing papers to be shut down by the regime. Most revealing has been the recent closure of conservative newspaper '9 Dey'. The Ministry of Islamic Culture and Guidance, currently headed by Ali Jannati, noted that this paper had violated a number of Iran's media laws by publishing highly critical articles about Iran's nuclear talks.

With no real clear boundaries of what will be censored, the Iranian Government also partakes in self-censorship. Most recently, newspapers have been banned from publishing photos or interviews of Iran's reformist politician Mohammad Khatami (he served as the president of Iran from 1997–2005). The effects of this have only served to highlight the unnecessary and absurd nature of Iran's censorship policy.

The effects of censorship are long-lasting, not only for those who suffer from it but also for the country itself. It leads to further divisions, lost culture and a drain of the country's most creative minds.

Their pens might be broken, but their words remain intact.

12

Librarians Must Resist Self-Censoring

Caitlin McCabe

Caitlin McCabe is an independent comics scholar and contributing editor to the Comic Book Legal Defense Fund.

The challenging and banning of books is a process that can be difficult for librarians, especially if it creates controversy within their communities. As a result, some librarians are resorting to a kind of self-censoring, when they decide not to order titles for their libraries that may create controversy. This might make things easier for them, but it is essentially a different type of censorship, and one that may be more difficult to deal with within a community.

It isn't just upset community members who contribute to book censorship. A recent Controversial Books Survey done by *School Library Journal* found that school librarians themselves are more likely now than they were eight years ago to add content warning labels, create restriction sections, or flat out not buy particular challenged books for their collections.

In a recap of survey results, Linda Jacobson discusses self-censorship on the library front as a means to avoid controversy within an increasingly reactive society.

In 2008, *SLJ* conducted a landmark survey that uncovered critical data about trends occurring at the school and library level with regard to book censorship. Looking at all levels of education,

"Survey Shows Stark Increase in Librarian Self-Censorship," by Caitlin McCabe, Comic Book Legal Defense Fund, October 7, 2016. Reprinted by permission.

from elementary school to high school, the survey examined how content labels were being applied to controversial books, how many librarians had constructed restricted sections for flagged titles, and even the frequency with which a librarian would simply pass on purchasing a particular title due to its content.

Although the findings were troubling, eight years later, things look a lot grimmer. Whereas in 2008 the use of content labels across elementary to high schools was an average of 11%, that number has jumped to 24% today—elementary and middle school libraries were impacted the most, with a 15% and 17% increase in flagging respectively.

A similar pattern has been uncovered for restricted sections, with 10% of elementary, 12% of middle school, and 6% of high school librarians saying that they have built restricted sections for mature or potentially controversial titles.

Most alarming, though, were the findings on book buying habits. More than 90% of elementary and middle school librarians commented that they decided not to buy books that could cause offense. High school librarians reported 75%.

"I used to not buy books where there was sex, but then I thought, 'if it [involves] a ghost that's 240 years old, I guess it's OK,'" notes Sara Stevenson, librarian at O. Henry Middle School in Austin, TX, adding:

> Then I had to change it to, 'OK, as long as it's just implied.' Then I had to change it to, 'OK, as long as it's not too graphic.' Then I had to let some more graphic ones through because the kids wanted them and they had great reviews. Now there are more and more books with gay sex, so where do you draw the line?

What is causing this alarming trend? Out of all of the 574 librarians surveyed, more that 40% noted that they had faced book challenges at their schools.

Organizations like CBLDF are kept busy defending books from challenges. From joining coalitions to defend popular books like TTYL and TTFN, as we did recently in Nassau County, Florida, to writing a letter to Virginia Governor Terry McAuliffe urging him to veto a house bill that would change the way that books are assigned and read in the state, free speech advocates, teachers, and librarians across the country are dealing with challenge situations that often make them resort to self-censroship to avoid controversy. "We can be our own worst enemies," continues Stevenson, who has dealt with challenges her whole career. "I fear I will be less brave now that I've had to go through the ordeal of a formal challenge."

One way to combat this fear is to establish clear and precise challenge policies within schools that allow teachers and librarians to have a structured method of dealing with an attempt to remove a book. Moreover as Pat Scales, the former chair of ALA's Intellectual Freedom Committee notes, conversation with concerned parents is also key. "Good conversation with a parent, or any challenger, usually ends with reason, and without further actions," she says.

The worst thing that can be done, though, is to deny children the right to materials because a few deem them to be too inappropriate. Contrary to adult beliefs, if children find a book too difficult, they will let you know that they are not ready for the material. Moreover, as Scales points out, if you allow them the flexibility to make choices about their reading material, you benefit on two fronts: you allow them access to texts that can help inform the broader world that they are living in, but also encourage them to explore their literary boundaries in a non-hostile manner. "When we free them to read, we also free them to reject," and at the end of the day it is their right to uninhibited education that should be protected.

13

Book Banning Is Irrelevant in the Information Age

Steven Petite

Steven Petite is a freelance writer whose work has appeared in many magazines. He has written extensively about books, video games, music, movies, television, sports, technology, and politics.

What has book banning looked like in the past, and what does it look like now? Some things haven't changed, with governments and individuals challenging books that they feel are inappropriate or politically threatening. But in this age of internet access, cell phones, and other digital media, information is more widely available and book banning, particularly with young people, is no longer as effective at controlling what children access.

L iterature is a wonderful and integral part of the human experience. Books have the power to teach us about ourselves and the world around us. They can open up doors to new ideas, new outlooks, and fresh experiences. The best books deal with complicated, important, and often times controversial topics. Literature can be beautiful and unsettling all at once. When a writer puts his/her inner thoughts on the page to comment about the world we live in, it is a gift for all people to learn from and enjoy. There is nothing more raw than honest words in the pages of a great novel. With that rawness and creative freedom, there

"Banning Books in the 21st Century," by Steven Petite, *Times Internet Limited*, June 5, 2015. Reprinted by permission.

comes a price. Certain groups and individuals view some works of literature as detrimental instead of a valuable addition to the world.

Book banning is not a new concept, as governments and educational institutions have been banning books in America since the 1600's. Defining books such as *The Great Gatsby, The Catcher in the Rye, To Kill a Mockingbird, Beloved,* 1984, *The Lord of the Flies, The Color Purple, The Grapes of Wrath,* and many others have been banned for various reasons. All of these books are also staples in American schools today and have been for many years. These books have undoubtedly inspired and changed countless amounts of lives from being taught as part of school curriculums. Banning books contradicts First Amendment Rights, but it does not stop groups from trying to ban certain works, even in today's saturated entertainment and technological world.

Parents of schools in Idaho and North Carolina currently want John Steinbeck's classic, *Of Mice and Men,* and Khaled Hosseini's modern triumph, *The Kite Runner,* banned from their respective high schools. *Of Mice and Men* is facing adversity due to coarse language and dark themes. While The Kite Runner is being accused of having too many adult themes and portraying women in a negative light.

As a book lover, this is undeniably outrageous. As a human being, this is incredibly disheartening knowing that the opportunity to learn about different cultures and times in an extremely beneficial and increasingly scarce art form, the written word, is being threatened by groups of misguided individuals.

Questions for the parents who want these books banned: Do your kids have cell phones? Access to the internet and social media? Video games? Cable television? If the answer is yes to any of those questions, then your kid is learning about the world already through less tasteful venues. They are forming their own views of the world around them based on what they watch on television and read on the internet, and it's likely that they are not getting the whole picture while being exposed to much more inappropriate material then they will ever read about in a piece of literature assigned in the classroom. Quite frankly, supporters of banning books are trying to steal from their child's education, place them in a bubble, and refrain from allowing them to see the world as it really was and is from different perspectives. All the while, either unbeknownst to them, or just unwilling to admit it, their children are already being exposed to exactly what they are trying to keep away from them.

Of Mice and Men shows a different time in an incredibly real light, that cannot be learned from modern day society. As they say, in order to not repeat the past, we must learn from it, and while the short novel has strong themes, it is a great tool for teaching about our past mistakes. *The Kite Runner* shows how life was and very much still is growing up in The Middle East. With so much tension between America and The Middle East, *The Kite Runner* is arguably one of the most important books to teach in classrooms today because it humanizes a region that some Americans have such disdain towards because of the minority portion of bad people who call that region home. If anything, it shows how lucky we are as a nation to have the rights that we have in a free world, and provides a means to empathize with an area that is still progressing towards equality and freedom for all.

Ironically, as an author, having a book banned, is usually a good thing for sales as well as notoriety. Banned books bring attention to the root problems whether the people advocating the ban realize it or not. Discussion commences on the major issues of the work in question, but banning them does not solve the problem. See, because the only way to truly shed light on the controversy is to read the book, to learn from its themes, and gain a new outlook on the world and how to make it better for everyone. Authors whose books have been banned by governments and in schools should feel a sense of pride since they created something that sparks a response. We owe it to the author to respond to the work by learning not avoiding the themes as a whole. If we act like the themes of banned books do not exist then we are denying the truth that the world was never perfect and it never will be. The best that we can do is take the time to read great pieces of literature, and form our own opinions on how change can arise. We should read and then act instead of not reading these books at all.

14

Technology Offers New Challenges to Censorship

Robert Wheaton

Robert Wheaton is a writer and the Chief Operating Officer at Penguin Random House Publishers in Canada.

Originally, books and other printed materials were the vehicles for disseminating ideas and viewpoints that might be censored or banned. But in this age of information, printed books have largely been superseded by digital media. Books themselves can now be accessed immediately as well, in digital format, and their distribution is much harder to control. With its ability to convey information almost instantaneously, the internet and other constantly-evolving forms of technological communication are fast becoming the new battlegrounds for controlling what can and cannot be accessed.

On Jan. 25, Twitter's website became inaccessible in Egypt. Protesters, who had gathered in Cairo's Tahrir Square and in other cities across the country, quickly responded by using proxies and other services to communicate with one another. The government moved the following day to restrict access to Google and to Facebook, where groups including We are all Khaled Said—founded by Google marketing executive Wael Ghonim—had become a key points for protesters to organize and share information.

"Banning Books in the Age of Information." by Robert Wheaton, The Huffington Post, December 1, 2011. Reprinted by permission.

On Jan. 27, the Egyptian government shut down the country's official Domain Name System, applied pressure to the country's four internet service providers, and took other measures to effectively disable the Internet for the entire country and sever it from the rest of the world.

The relationship between power and information has always been taut and laced with danger. It has always pushed the boundaries of technology. During the Reformation, illegal publications circulated along the river trade routes of Europe alongside an explosion in literacy and the spread of the printing press. The social and intellectual unrest associated with this information revolution plunged a continent into decades of war and revolution.

We are living through a change in communications technology every bit as extensive as the invention of movable type, with far-reaching implications for censorship and the control of ideas.

With the explosion of digital reading, governments and institutions seeking to outlaw books are no longer just confronted with the logistical challenges: how to intimidate publishers and distributors; how to restrain booksellers; how to inspect goods at borders; how to destroy confiscated copies. The terrain now includes Internet Service Providers and hard drives, remote servers and peer-to-peer file-sharing networks, international eBook retailers and libraries with extensive digital collections. As all these mechanisms of digital reading expand, it will become much, much harder for authorities to ban books or otherwise prevent people from reading them. Books can be distributed in seconds, and read from devices that do not display their contents across the front and can even be password-protected.

These new circumstances apply to state governments working against political sedition, to school boards and municipal authorities attempting to influence the reading materials of increasingly tech-savvy teenagers.

As a result, those wishing to combat censorship have powerful tools at their disposal. When a Missouri school board banned Kurt Vonnegut's *Slaughterhouse Five*, the Vonnegut Memorial Library offered free copies to students. Imagine the same scenario taking place electronically, instantaneously distributing copies to a select or a general audience.

Instant distribution also dramatically expands the power of word of mouth. Often the banning of books takes place less to prevent the actual reading of a book, but instead as an opportunity for a person or a body to establish their own political, social, cultural, or moral position. It's a publicity stunt, a way for a politician, school board, or a government to show that they are not in favour of the politics or lifestyle expressed in a book. An ambitious young district attorney might seek to limit the importation of a *Howl*, or *Ulysses*, or *The God of Small Things*, in order to make a name for themselves ahead of an election.

There is an implicit gamble here: that the extra publicity adhering to the cited book may drive readers' desire to read it, but if the physical distribution of that book is limited—by power, coercion, influence, or simply by supply chain realities—the authority can receive more coverage than the book it is rejecting. People simply won't be able to get a copy of the book in question— and in the meantime the would-be censors have defined themselves in the public mind, raising funding or winning elections with the support of those that agree.

But in a world where technologies allow one-click circulation of information—instantaneously, impulsively, and across borders— that gamble is now lopsided. An extra dose of publicity—and word-of-mouth power of social media—can lead to an unlimited amount of distribution for the book in question.

This isn't a panacea: eBooks are subject to the digital divide every bit as much as the Internet at large. Access to information remains highly uneven depending on socio-economic circumstance. Initiatives like One Laptop per Child are making progress at combating this inequality, but in many parts of the world authority retains the upper hand over information. And literacy itself remains a real and present constraint upon the spread of ideas in the world.

Moreover, the potential for tracking reading remains more acute for digital reading. With physical books, evidence can always be destroyed or hidden, without leaving a trace in your digital purchase history or the activities associated with your IP address. In the future, having failed to fully erased an ePub file from your hard drive, or to have masked your IP address accessing a P2P service, may be the 21st-century equivalent of, in different times and places, being caught with a copy of *The Satanic Verses* or *Uncle Tom's Cabin* buried in your back yard. Evidence of having read a book is no longer simply its residence in your imagination.

In the weeks following the fall of Egyptian President Hosni Mubarak, thousands of books banned in previous decades became available again. Booksellers even offered customers discounts on books that had been unavailable for years. Reader interest that was dammed up for years was unleashed as soon as physical copies could be printed and distributed around the country. In the future, these waters may not be so easily regulated—and the currents may be turbulent for all.

15

Why Book Banning Fails

Philip Nel

Philip Nel is a professor of English and directs the graduate program in Children's Literature at Kansas State University. He is co-editor of Tales for Little Rebels: A Collection of Radical Children's Literature (2008) and Keywords for Children's Literature (2011).

While many books are banned because they are deemed inappropriate for young readers, the books that are banned reflect the fears of adults, and not the fears of children themselves. Banning books cannot keep children safe, whereas open discussions about the issues they contain can prepare children to face the situations they will encounter in their own lives. Restricting these books can deny children and teens the access to the books that would benefit them the most, and help allay their own fears.

Few things upset American adults more than books for children and adolescents. If you look at the American Library Association's annual list of Challenged and Banned Books, the top 10 titles are nearly always those written for or assigned to young people: J.K. Rowling's Harry Potter novels, Dav Pilkey's Captain Underpants series, Mark Twain's *Adventures of Huckleberry Finn*, Toni Morrison's *The Bluest Eye*. On those rare occasions when the books are not intended for school-age readers or given as homework, they're on the list because young people are reading

"Innocent Children and Frightened Adults: Why Censorship Fails," by Philip Nel, September 30, 2015. Reprinted by permission.

them anyway: E.L. James' *Fifty Shades of Grey*, a favorite target for 2012 and 2013.

Banned and challenged books tell us very little about what is suitable for actual children. Instead, books targeted for censure offer an index of adult fears, reflecting, as David Booth says, "changing ideas about childhood and notions of suitability."[1] Censorship is also transideological, advocated by people of many political persuasions. Progressive censors seek to scrub away racism from *Doctor Dolittle* and *Huckleberry Finn*, creating Bowdlerized editions of the books. Conservative censors wish to protect children from knowledge of the human body: as a result, Robie Harris and Michael Emberley's *It's Perfectly Normal: Changing Bodies, Growing Up, Sex, and Sexual Health* frequently lands on the ALA's Challenged-and-Banned Books list.

While censorship will not keep young people safe, censors and would-be censors are right about two things. First, books have power. Second, responsible adults should help guide young people through the hazards of the adult world.

However, like all attempts to safeguard children's innocence, removing books from libraries and curricula are not only doomed to failure; they are an abdication of adult responsibility and, as Marah Gubar writes of associating innocence with childhood, "potentially damaging to the wellbeing of actual young people."[2] A responsible adult recognizes that innocence is a negative state—an absence of knowledge and experience—and thus cannot be sustained. Shielding children from books that offer insight into the world's dangers puts these children at risk. As Meg Rosoff notes, "If you don't talk to kids about the difficult stuff, they worry alone."[3] Books offer a safe space in which to have conversations about difficult subjects. Taking these books out of circulation diminishes understanding and increases anxiety.

Separating children from books also fails to recognize that peril is not distributed randomly throughout the population, but concentrated in groups identifiable by their members' race, gender, class, sexuality, disability, or religion. Preventing teenagers from reading Laurie Halse Anderson's *Speak* or Maya Angelou's *I Know Why the Caged Bird Sings* impedes them from learning about what survivors of rape endure, and how peers and teachers might better help them. Blocking children from reading Justin Richardson, Peter Parnell, and Henry Cole's *And Tango Makes Three* prevents them from understanding that same-sex parents appear elsewhere in the animal kingdom, too. Banning Tim O'Brien's *The Things They Carried* and Walter Dean Myers's *Fallen Angels* stops readers from discovering how war shapes a young psyche. Prohibiting Sherman Alexie's *The Absolutely True Story of a Part-Time Indian* impedes young people from learning about the hard realities of life on a reservation, and from getting to know the novel's resilient, funny protagonist. These books provide mirrors for young people of similar backgrounds or experiences, and windows for those of different ones.

Furthermore, preventing children from reckoning with potentially offensive works ill prepares them for the indignities that life will inflict. They should read books that trouble them, and have serious conversations about those books. For example, while Twain was a progressive nineteenth-century white author, if his *Huckleberry Finn* doesn't offend contemporary readers, then they're not reading it carefully enough. It's not just the repeated use of the n-word, which should make people at least uncomfortable and at most angry (news flash: it was a racial slur in the nineteenth century, too). The portrayal of slave-owning Uncle Silas as a kindly "old gentleman" (Huck calls him "the innocentest, best old soul I ever see") offers an apology for white supremacy. Assigning Huck Finn provides an occasion not only to talk about a classic American novel, but to teach people how to read uncomfortably, and to cope with experiences that upset them.

Though the motive is protection, restricting access to books hurts the children and teens who need them most. Young readers in vulnerable populations crave stories that help them make sense of their lives. Denying them access to these books contributes to their marginalization and puts them at greater risk. In any case, children often have experiences that they do not yet have the words to express: reading books can provide them with the words, and help them better understand. As Mr. Antolini tells Holden Caulfield in J.D. Salinger's *The Catcher in the Rye* (another frequently challenged book), "you'll find that you're not the first person who was ever confused and frightened and even sickened by human behavior.… Many, many men have been just as troubled morally and spiritually as you are right now. Happily, some of them kept records of their troubles. You'll learn from them—if you want to."[4]

Young people do want to learn. Concerned adults should acknowledge innocence's inevitable evaporation, and recognize that the young likely know more than you think they do. So, respect their curiosity. Take their concerns seriously. Let them read. Let them learn.

Notes

1. David Booth, "Censorship," Keywords for Children's Literature, eds. Philip Nel and Lissa Paul (NYU Press, 2011), p. 26.
2. Marah Gubar, "Innocence," Keywords for Children's Literature, eds. Nel and Paul, p. 122.
3. Meg Rosoff, "You can't protect children by lying to them—the truth will hurt less." The Guardian 20 Sept. 2013: <http://www.theguardian.com/lifeandstyle/2013/sep/21/cant-protect-children-by-lying>.
4. J.D. Salinger, The Catcher in the Rye (1951; Bantam Books, 1988), p. 189.

Organizations to Contact

The editors have compiled the following list of organizations concerned with the issues debated in this book. The descriptions are derived from materials provided by the organizations. All have publications or information available for interested readers. The list was compiled on the date of publication of the present volume; the information provided here may change. Be aware that many organizations take several weeks or longer to respond to inquiries, so allow as much time as possible.

American Library Association
50 East Huron Street
Chicago, IL 60611-2795
800-545-2433
email: ala@ala.org
website: http://www.ala.org

The American Library Association's mission is to provide leadership for the development, promotion, and improvement of library and information services and the profession of librarianship in order to enhance learning and ensure access to information for all.

American Society of Journalists and Authors
355 Lexington Avenue, 15th Floor
New York, NY 10017-6603
212-997-0947
email: asjaoffice@asja.org
website: http://asja.org/

Founded in 1948, the American Society of Journalists and Authors is the nation's professional organization of independent nonfiction writers. The organization offers a variety of benefits and services to its members and is a leader in the establishment of professional and ethical standards in the publishing community.

Freedom to Read Foundation
50 East Huron St.
Chicago, IL 60611
1-800-545-2433 ext 4226
email: ftrf@ala.org
website: www.ftrf.org

The Freedom to Read Foundation (FTRF) is a non-profit legal and educational organization affiliated with the American Library Association. FTRF protects and defends the First Amendment to the Constitution and supports the right of libraries to collect—and individuals to access—information.

National Coalition Against Censorship (NCAC)
19 Fulton Street, Suite 407
New York, NY 10038
212-807-6222
email: ncac@ncac.org
website: http://ncac.org/

Formed in 1975, NCAC's mission is to promote freedom of thought, inquiry and expression and oppose censorship in all its forms. NCAC supports First Amendment principals by engaging in advocacy and education in alliance with more than 50 national non-profits.

National Council of Teachers of English
1111 W. Kenyon Road
Urbana, IL 61801-1096
Phone: 217-328-3870 or 877-369-6283
website: http://www.ncte.org/

The National Council of Teachers of English is devoted to improving the teaching and learning of English and the language arts at all levels of education. The Council promotes the development of literacy, the use of language to construct personal and public worlds and to achieve full participation in society, through the learning and teaching of English and the related arts and sciences of language.

PEN America
588 Broadway, Suite 303
New York, NY 10012
212-334-1660
email: info@pen.org
website: http://pen.org/

PEN America supports the freedom to write and unites writers and their allies to celebrate creative expression and defend the liberties that make it possible. PEN America is committed to defending the freedom that makes creative expression possible. PEN America works with the international PEN community to ensure the freedom to create, convey information and ideas, and for those ideas to be accessed by others.

People for the American Way
1101 15th Street, NW, Suite 600
Washington, DC 20005
1-800-326-7329
email: pfaw@pfaw.org
website: http://www.pfaw.org/

People For the American Way is a progressive advocacy organizations founded to fight right-wing extremism and defend constitutional values under attack, including free expression, religious liberty, equal justice under the law, and the right to meaningfully participate in our democracy.

Project Censored
P.O. Box 750940
Petaluma, CA 94975
707-874-2695
website: http://projectcensored.org/

Project Censored educates students and the public about the importance of a truly free press for democratic self-government by exposing and opposing news censorship and promoting independent investigative journalism, media literacy, and critical thinking.

Bibliography

Books

Scott Barbour. *Opposing Viewpoints: Censorship*. New York, NY: Greenhaven Publishing, 2010.

Roberta Baxter. *The Bill of Rights*. Portsmouth, NH: Heinemann, 2012.

Robert P. Doyle. *Banned Books: Challenging Our Freedom to Read*. Chicago, IL: American Library Association, 2014.

Carolee Laine. *Book Banning and Other Forms of Censorship*. North Mankato, MN: Essential Library, 2016.

ReLeah Cossett Lent and Gloria Pipkin. *Keep Them Reading: An Anti-Censorship Handbook for Educators*. New York, NY: Teachers College Press, 2012.

Nicholas J. Karolides. *120 Banned Books: Censorship Histories of World Literature,* 2nd Edition. New York, NY: Checkmark Books, 2011.

Trina Magi. *Intellectual Freedom Manual*, Ninth Edition. Chicago, IL: American Library Association, 2015.

Catherine J. Ross. *Lessons in Censorship: How Schools and Courts Subvert Students' First Amendment Rights*. Cambridge, MA: Harvard University Press, 2015.

Pat R. Scales. *Books under Fire: A Hit List of Banned and Challenged Children's Books*. Chicago, IL: American Library Association, 2015.

Pat R. Scales. *Defending Frequently Challenged Young Adult Books: A Handbook for Librarians and Educators*. Lanham, MD: Rowman & Littlefield, 2016.

Paul Von Blum. *Censorship*. San Diego, CA: Cognella Academic Publishing, 2010.

Periodicals and Internet Sources

American Library Association, "Timeline: 30 Years of Liberating Literature." http://www.ala.org/bbooks/ frequentlychallengedbooks/timeline.

Banned Books Week, "Banned Books That Shaped America," http://www.bannedbooksweek.org/censorship/ bannedbooksthatshapedamerica.

Sarah Begley, "What the List of Most Banned Books Says About Our Society's Fears," *Time Magazine*, September 25, 2016. http://time.com/4505713/banned-books-week-reasons-change.

Book and Periodical Council of Canada, "Bannings and Burnings in History," Freedom to Read. http://www. freedomtoread.ca/links-and-resources/bannings-and-burnings-in-history/#.WIZqyFxhOVA.

Amy Brady, "The History (and Present) of Banning Books in America," Literary Hub, September 22, 2016. http:// lithub.com/the-history-and-present-of-banning-books-in-america.

Clay Calvert, "Why Are Libraries Still Banning Books?" *Newsweek*, October 5, 2015. http://www.newsweek.com/ how-come-libraries-are-still-banning-books-379958.

Cristen Conger, "How Book Banning Works," How Stuff Works, http://people.howstuffworks.com/book-banning.htm.

Mark Hemingway, "In Defense of Book Banning," *The Federalist*, March 11, 2014. http://thefederalist. com/2014/03/11/in-defense-of-book-banning/.

Mette Newth, "The Long History of Censorship," Beacon for Freedom of Expression, 2010. http://www. beaconforfreedom.org/liste.html?tid=415&art_id=475.

People for the American Way, "Schools and Censorship: Banned Books," October 2008, People for the American

Way. http://www.pfaw.org/report/schools-and-censorship-banned-books.

Paul Ringel, "How Banning Books Marginalizes Children," *The Atlantic*, October 1, 2016. http://www.theatlantic.com/entertainment/archive/2016/10/how-banned-books-marginalize-children/502424

Annie Julia Wyman, "What Kind of Town Bans Books?" *The New Yorker*, October 1, 2015. http://www.newyorker.com/books/page-turner/what-kind-of-town-bans-books.

Index